YOU CHOOSE BOOKS

SPACE RACE

An Interactive Space Exploration Adventure

by Rebecca Stefoff

Consultant:
Richard Bell, PhD
Associate Professor of History
University of Maryland, College Park

CAPSTONE PRESS
a capstone imprint

You Choose Books are published by Capstone Press,
1710 Roe Crest Drive, North Mankato, Minnesota 56003
www.mycapstone.com

Library of Congress Cataloging-in-Publication Data
Names: Stefoff, Rebecca, 1951– author.
Title: Space race : an interactive space exploration adventure / by Rebecca
    Stefoff.
Description: North Mankato, Minnesota : You Choose Books, an imprint of
    Capstone Press, [2017] | Series: You choose books. You choose. Space |
    Audience: Ages 8–12. | Audience: Grades 4 to 6. | Includes
    bibliographical references and index.
Identifiers: LCCN 2016009144| ISBN 9781491481011 (library binding) | ISBN
    9781491481363 (pbk.) | ISBN 9781491481400 (ebook (pdf))
Subjects: LCSH: Space race—History—Juvenile literature. | Space flight to
    the moon—History—Juvenile literature. |
    Moon—Exploration—History—Juvenile literature. | Outer
    space—Exploration—History—Juvenile literature.
Classification: LCC TL788.5 .S74 2017 | DDC 629.4/109046—dc23
LC record available at http://lccn.loc.gov/2016009144

Editorial Credits
Adrian Vigliano, editor; Kayla Rossow, designer;
Wanda Winch, media researcher; Laura Manthe, production specialist

Photo Credits
AP Images, 89; Getty Images: UIG/Sovfoto, 6; NASA, 12, 17, 36, 50, 105, Dryden
Flight Research Center, 28, 40, ESA/Hubble Heritage Team (STScI/AURA),
nebula design element, Johnson Space Center, cover, 23, 30, 44, 62, 67, 69, 82, 99,
100, 103, Marshall Space Flight Center, 10; National Naval Aviation Museum
Library: Robert Lawson Photograph Collection, 72; Naval Heritage & History
Command: photo by Milt Putnam, HS-4, 92 [UA 44.02.01]; Newscom: CNP/
NASA, 77; Shutterstock: HelenField, lunar surface design, HorenkO, paper design

Printed in Canada.
009634F16

Table of Contents

ABOUT YOUR
ADVENTURE

YOU are living in the mid-1900s. The world's two rival superpowers each want to be first into a new frontier: space. But space is full of hazards. Sending a machine, animal, or person into it will take skill, hard work, and daring.

In this book you'll explore how the choices people made meant the difference between life and death. The events you'll experience happened to real people.

Chapter One sets the scene. Then you choose which path to read. Follow the directions at the bottom of each page. The choices you make will change your outcome. After you finish your path, go back and read the others for new perspectives and more adventures.

YOU CHOOSE the path
you take through history.

In July 1950 the Bumper 2 became the first rocket launched from Cape Canaveral, Florida. Bumper 2 was designed using technology from the V-2 missiles of World War II.

CHAPTER 1

THE RACE BEGINS

You are living in a time of change and scientific progress. Ever since World War II ended in 1945, nations have been rebuilding. Some are making incredible leaps in science and technology. But the most exciting new frontier lies just ahead. Governments and scientists are working to begin the exploration of space. With great excitement, you watch the race to space begin.

7

Turn the page.

The space race has roots in World War II. One power in that conflict was Nazi Germany, which poured money and engineers into developing rockets for use in war. Germany was defeated by a group of nations that included the United States, Great Britain, and the Soviet Union. Afterward, the United States and the Soviet Union each acquired German rocket technology and scientists. The United States got Germany's powerful V-2 missile, along with rocketry expert Wernher von Braun, who was interested in space exploration.

A key part of the space race is the Cold War between the United States and the Soviet Union, which started in the late 1940s. The two nations were allies in World War II, but have become rivals. Now they are the world's superpowers. Each tries to gain influence over other countries around the globe. The conflict between the United States and the Soviet Union is called a "cold" war because open warfare has never quite broken out between them.

Americans fear the spread of Soviet communism. Leaders also worry about the growing military strength of the Soviet Union— especially after the Soviets test their first atomic bomb in 1949. When it becomes clear that the Soviets are building atomic bombs to compete with those controlled by the United States, many Americans fear that these atomic weapons will be turned against them.

Turn the page.

10

Wernher von Braun (arm in cast) and a group of other German rocket scientists surrendered to American soldiers on May 2, 1945.

The United States and the Soviet Union start stockpiling atomic weapons. They are also developing long-range rockets to carry weapons across an ocean in case of war. Engineer Sergei Korolev heads a Soviet rocketry program. Von Braun heads the American program.

Both nations see space as the next frontier. Satellites in orbit around Earth could be used for communications, spying, scientific research, and maybe for launching weapons. In July 1955 the United States says that it will launch an Earth-orbiting satellite in the next few years. Four days later the Soviet Union says the same thing. Which nation will be first in space? The space race is on—and you can be part of it.

To help the United States get into space by working as an engineer, turn to page 13.

To be among the first women to be tested for the U.S. space program, turn to page 43.

To become a cosmonaut with a chance to travel into space for the Soviet Union, turn to page 71.

Wernher von Braun (left) and Willy Ley (right) worked with Disney to make "Man in Space." This 1955 TV episode helped a large audience understand spaceflight.

CHAPTER 2

A GREAT TIME TO BE AN ENGINEER

"Daddy, can we watch *Disneyland?*"

"Sure, kids," you say. "We'll watch together."

When you turn on the TV set, the blank screen becomes a black-and-white picture. The kids' faces light up. To a six-year-old and an eight-year-old, it must seem like magic. As an electrical engineer, you know better. But tonight is for fun, not for explaining how a TV works.

Disneyland aired about six months ago, in the fall of 1954. You smile when you see the title of tonight's show: "Man in Space." You've loved the idea of space travel since you were a teenager.

Turn the page.

Dr. Willy Ley appears, talking about someday sending people into space using rocket-driven ships. You admire Ley, a science writer who fled his native Germany in 1935 to escape the Nazi party. You have different feelings about another guest, Dr. Wernher von Braun. He is one of the world's top experts on rocket science and a believer in human space exploration. But von Braun was once a member of the Nazi Party, the enemy of the United States in World War II. He led the German program to build military rockets during the war.

Seeing von Braun on your television screen brings unwelcome memories of the time you spent serving in the U.S. Army in Europe during the war. After the war, you studied engineering. Now, with a master's degree in electrical engineering, you work for a company that designs parts for airplanes.

The next week you receive an unexpected job offer. At the U.S. Army's Redstone Arsenal, in Alabama, scientists and engineers are creating new versions of the German V-2 missile. They need an electrical engineer with experience designing aircraft equipment. It would mean moving your family, but you would be working in rocket science. However, the head of the program is Wernher von Braun. Could you work for him?

Scientists worked in teams to assemble rockets at Redstone.

To say no, turn to page 16.
To say yes and join the Redstone team, turn to page 23.

You turn down the job in Alabama. But a few months later, you worry that you missed a chance to be part of a great adventure.

The evening TV news on July 29, 1955, includes a surprising announcement. President Dwight D. Eisenhower wants the United States to launch "a small Earth-circling satellite" as early as the middle of 1957. Humankind's first step into space could be just a couple of years away!

Four days later another startling announcement comes, this time by a Soviet scientist. He says that the Soviet Union will place a satellite into Earth orbit in the near future. Unlike the Americans, the Soviets don't say that their satellites will be for scientific research. It's no secret that any country's rockets and satellites could have military uses.

The world's two rival superpowers have staked claims to the frontier beyond Earth's atmosphere. It's a space race—and you're sure that von Braun's team is in the middle of it.

President Eisenhower, however, has a different idea. He wants the first U.S. step into space to come from a civilian project. This will show that America's goals in space are scientific, not military. The Naval Research Laboratory (NRL) is staffed by civilians who are working on a rocket called Vanguard. Eisenhower says that Vanguard, not von Braun's Redstone, will carry the U.S. satellites into space.

Turn the page.

A few days later your boss at the aircraft design company offers you a supervisor's job. It would mean managing people instead of designing electrical gear, but it would bring a bigger salary and a promotion. You tell him you will think it over, but you are pretty sure you will say yes.

The very next day you get a job offer from the Vanguard rocket team. It's your second chance to be part of the space race, but it won't pay as well as the supervisor's job. The Vanguard job would also mean a move to Cape Canaveral, the U.S. Air Force base in Florida where rockets are tested.

To join the Vanguard team, go to page 19.
To become a supervisor at your company, turn to page 34.

You and your family love Florida's beaches and palm trees. Even better, you like working on the Vanguard rocket.

It's a three-stage rocket. The first stage, at the bottom, is an engine and the fuel that it will burn to lift the rocket off the launchpad. That stage will drop away once its fuel is used. Then the engine in the second stage will fire. It also will drop off once it's empty. The engine in the third stage will be left to carry a three-pound, grapefruit-sized satellite into orbit.

You work on the second stage, which contains telemetry equipment. These instruments gather information about the rocket's flight, such as its speed and altitude. They send the information by radio to mission controllers on Earth. Your job is to make sure the electrical circuits that power the instruments stand up to the force of launch.

Turn the page.

By early October 1957, the rocket has passed two test launches. Soon the team will be ready to send up the satellite. Then, on October 4, you and the other engineers are stunned by news that spreads through Cape Canaveral.

The Soviet Union has successfully launched the first artificial satellite to orbit Earth. Called Sputnik 1, it circles the planet every 98 minutes. All over the world, people with radio sets hear the "beep beep beep" that Sputnik beams out.

Americans are shocked at being beaten to this first space goal. They also worry about what the Soviets might do in space. Orders go out to the Vanguard program to get an American satellite into space right away.

You and the team work many hours trying to catch up. You are sure Vanguard's telemetry will work, but before you can find out, you get another shock. The Soviets have launched a second satellite, Sputnik 2, carrying the first passenger to orbit Earth—a dog named Laika.

Finally, on December 6, 1957, everything is ready for Vanguard's first attempt to launch a satellite. The launch is being shown live on television, but you and other project workers are there in person—at a safe distance. Your heart pounds with excitement and pride. Soon the rocket will climb into the sky on a trail of fire.

With a loud, deep rumble the rocket rises—and falls back to the ground after climbing just a few feet. The fuel tanks explode. The rocket is destroyed. The satellite beams out its signal, but from the ground, not from orbit.

Turn the page.

The failure is a huge embarrassment. The Soviets publicly offer to help the United States with its space program. American journalists give mocking nicknames to the failed satellite, calling it Dudnik, Flopnik, and Kaputnik.

You decide to look for another job. You make a few calls and learn that there's room for you at the Redstone Arsenal in Alabama.

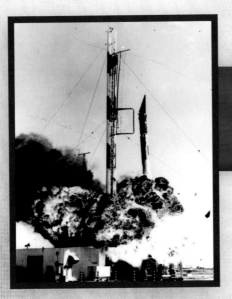

The Vanguard rocket exploded during the launch attempt.

To work for von Braun, go to page 23.
To look for a different career, turn to page 36.

In Huntsville, Alabama, you work on the enormous military base where rockets are designed and built. The growth of the Redstone Arsenal's rocket program has drawn people like you from all over the country. Huntsville's nickname is Rocket City.

You work for the Army Ballistic Missile Agency (ABMA), which employs both military scientists and civilians. Its director is Wernher von Braun. "Will I work closely with him?" you ask Corporal Wilkins, who handles your hiring. Wilkins tells you that von Braun is far above your level and is always busy. He oversees several rocket-development programs and travels a lot.

Turn the page.

You will work under one of ABMA's many head engineers. "There are many rocket programs here," Wilkins says. "All of them use Redstone rockets, based on the V-2s that Dr. von Braun worked on in Germany. We've been flight-testing Redstones since 1953, but now the teams are taking them in different directions."

He offers you a choice. In one job, you'll work on the PGM-11. "This Redstone missile is key to our national defense right now," Wilkins explains. "There's a lot of government funding pouring into it." The other position involves a different spin-off of the Redstone called the Jupiter-C. "This rocket has potential for satellite launches," he says, "but there's no definite timetable."

To work on the PGM-11 missile, go to page 25.
To work on the Jupiter-C rocket, turn to page 30.

Corporal Wilkins called the PGM-11 a missile, not a rocket. A missile is something that is designed to hit a target. The PGM-11 will be the country's first large ballistic missile. A powerful engine in the lower section will launch the rocket into the atmosphere, then separate. The upper section, which is the actual missile, will continue to its target. Its path will be set by the downward pull of gravity and the drag of the atmosphere.

Turn the page.

Your job is to design and test the electrical circuits that control the connections between the lower and upper sections. The two parts must separate at just the right moment, after the engine stops firing. If they don't, the weight of the lower section will pull the missile off course, and it will miss its target.

The PGM-11 was developed from the German V-2 missile of World War II.

"What do you think they'll use these missiles for?" you ask Stanton Riggs, a senior engineer in your department.

"It's a surface-to-surface missile," he replies. "Meant to be launched from ground level at a ground target." Riggs adds, "It can travel up to about 200 miles (322 kilometers). My guess is that we'll send these things to Europe."

You know what he means. The United States is locked in a Cold War with the Soviet Union. From its center in Russia, on the eastern edge of Europe, the Soviet Union has established fortified borders around the countries it controls. U.S. allies in Europe count on American military power to protect them if the Soviets attack.

Turn the page.

On January 31, 1958, a Juno-1 rocket—an offshoot of the Jupiter-C, developed by the team you didn't join—does what the earlier Vanguard project failed to do. It successfully launches the first U.S. satellite, Explorer 1, into orbit. Almost four months after Sputnik, the United States is finally in space!

You cheer along with everyone else in Rocket City, but you also feel some regret. You feel the same way two months later, when another Juno carries the second U.S. satellite into orbit.

In late July, Riggs tells you to pack your bags. The PGM-11 is going for a top-secret test, and you are part of the engineering crew for its final check-up. You must sign a paper stating that you won't discuss the test with anyone, even your wife. Your destination is a remote Pacific island. This can mean only one thing.

The United States has been testing atomic weapons on Pacific islands for several years. The bombs have been set off from the ground or from barges. Now, in a test code-named Hardtack Teak, your PGM-11 will be the first U.S. ballistic missile to be launched with a live atomic weapon.

You are on a Navy ship outside the blast zone when the missile is launched over Johnston Island on July 31, 1958. It rises to a height of 250,000 feet (76,200 meters). The warhead explodes as planned. After a blinding flash, an enormous mushroom-shaped cloud rises into the sky.

The soldiers and engineers around you are cheering and clapping, but you feel horrified. You didn't become an engineer to increase the chance of atomic war. Should you move to a Redstone group that is working on space launches? Or should you leave the field of rocketry altogether?

To move to a different Redstone team, turn to page 30.
To leave rocketry, turn to page 37.

You join the group working on the Jupiter-C rocket at the Redstone Arsenal. Late 1958 is an important time for space exploration.

That summer, President Eisenhower had created the National Aeronautics and Space Administration (NASA) to oversee space-related programs. NASA becomes active on October 1, which is also your first day on a new team called Project Mercury. Its goal is putting an American astronaut into orbit around Earth.

The Multiple Axis Space Test Inertia Facility (MASTIF) trained Mercury astronauts to control a spacecraft that could move in many directions at once.

The spacecraft that will carry the astronaut is called a capsule. An aircraft company in St. Louis, Missouri, is designing and building it. Your job involves electrical systems on the rocket that will launch the capsule into space. You are one of thousands of people working under Robert Gilruth, head of NASA's Space Task Group.

You and your coworkers know the United States and the Soviet Union are racing to send a person into space. The race becomes more urgent in 1959, after a Soviet spacecraft—without passengers—is the first to reach the moon and photograph the side that's never seen from Earth. The Soviets are racking up a lot of space firsts. Some Americans say that Eisenhower and NASA have ruined the United States' chance to win the space race.

Turn the page.

In October 1959 a coworker slaps a copy of *Newsweek* magazine onto your desk. Under the headline "How to Lose the Space Race!" a writer warns, "The U.S. is losing the race into space, and thus its predominance in the world."

"All of Gilruth's people are working 50 and 60 hours a week," you say. "We'll show them!"

In July 1960 NASA opens a new research facility, the Marshall Space Flight Center, at the Redstone Arsenal. Wernher von Braun is its director. Meanwhile, pressure is growing for a Mercury-Redstone launch. Finally, an unmanned capsule is scheduled to launch November 7. The rocket, MR-1, is shipped to Cape Canaveral in Florida. You travel there with the launch team.

On launch day, there's a problem with a gas tank that helps steer the capsule. The mission is rescheduled for November 21.

You attend a meeting to review the rocket's electrical systems. The group looks at a diagram of the circuit that carries electrical power from the launchpad to the booster rocket. You designed this circuit, which has performed perfectly on many military Redstones.

"Look at this plug," an engineer says. "One prong is longer than the other." He points to a plug that fastens a ground cable into the booster. It's designed to pull out of its socket when the rocket lifts up.

"There's never been a problem with it," you say. But the MR isn't an ordinary Redstone. If something goes wrong, it could be a disaster. But changing the plug now could cause another launch delay.

To say nothing, turn to page 38.
To suggest that the plug be changed, turn to page 40.

"I'm not sure it's a good idea to move to Florida," your wife says. "The kids are doing well in school, and their grandparents are here."

"You're right. But still," you say, "imagine being part of a space launch!"

On February 20, 1962, the Mercury program sent John Glenn into space. Glenn became the first American astronaut to orbit the Earth.

She smiles and places a hand on your shoulder. "I know how much that would mean to you. But maybe you should take that promotion. You see, I have some news, too. We're going to have another baby."

You hug her. Space suddenly seems like a distant dream.

The next day you tell your boss, "I'll take that supervisor job."

In the years that follow, like millions of people around the world, you watch the space race on your television screen. You may not be part of the space race, but you make sure that your three children get to see it.

THE END

To follow another path, turn to page 11.
To read the conclusion, turn to page 101.

Once you start looking for a new job, you realize that 1958 is a great time to be an engineer. Your skill in designing electrical circuits is in high demand.

Medical telemetry is a brand-new field. It is creating equipment to record patients' life signs, such as heart rate and breathing, and send that information to their doctors. Your work on satellite telemetry gives you an advantage. You go to work for a new company that's inventing tools to monitor heart activity. This field is bound to grow.

36

Best of all, you are still part of the space race. You don't work on rockets or satellites, but the medical telemetry you design will soon be used on animals and people who travel into space.

THE END

To follow another path, turn to page 11.
To read the conclusion, turn to page 101.

Back in Huntsville, you tell your family that you've decided to start a new career. Although you can't tell your wife about the atomic test, you think she understands. Together you decide to return to your hometown of Chicago.

Your mother, a retired teacher, suggests you try teaching. You like her idea and find a job teaching electrical engineering to college students. For 20 years you teach students skills they'll use in architecture, city planning, and computer science. Then you are diagnosed with cancer.

As you lie dying in your hospital bed, you wonder whether radiation from that atomic test years ago caused your cancer. You also wonder how many others were affected by the tests.

THE END

To follow another path, turn to page 11.
To read the conclusion, turn to page 101.

On November 21 crowds and camera crews gather to watch the MR-1 launch. The booster rocket's engine fires. With a mighty roar the rocket rises a few inches from the pad and then sinks back down. The capsule's emergency parachutes open, covering the stalled rocket.

The failed MR-1 launch became known as the "four-inch flight."

The crew discovers that the plug with two different prongs caused the launch failure. The plug worked on an ordinary Redstone rocket, but the capsule made the MR-1 heavier, so it rose a tiny bit more slowly. The two prongs should have disconnected from the circuit at the same time. On the MR-1, the shorter prong disconnected just 21 thousandths of a second before the longer one. That made the engine cut off.

You feel sick. As an engineer you know that the tiniest details matter. You should have said something.

Your bosses at NASA agree. You lose your job. A few days later you're back in Huntsville, explaining to your family that you'll be moving again soon.

THE END

To follow another path, turn to page 11.
To read the conclusion, turn to page 101.

"I think we should change that plug," you say. The room falls silent, and everyone stares at you.

"You said it's performed perfectly many times before," one of the senior engineers points out.

"Yes, but what if the rocket behaves differently with the capsule on top of it?"

Members of the group exchange glances. Finally the team leader says, "It would mean another launch delay while we run tests. I don't want to take that message to the top people. Do you?"

You shake your head.

"I say we stick to the schedule," the leader says, "You should have said something earlier."

You still think it would be smart to change the plug, but the decision is out of your hands.

Launch day is a disaster. The rocket rises just four inches before an electrical problem—caused by the uneven prongs—kills the engine. The rocket and capsule are damaged but can be repaired. What about your reputation?

Fortunately, other members of the electrical engineering team speak up for you. They tell the project directors that you suggested changing the plug but your team leader overruled you.

"We learn something important from every failure," your boss says back in Huntsville. "Now we're that much closer to sending one of our astronauts into space." You're happy to continue that adventure.

THE END

To follow another path, turn to page 11.
To read the conclusion, turn to page 101.

Geraldine "Jerrie" Cobb was an accomplished pilot by age 16. She later became the first woman to go through the testing developed for Mercury astronauts.

CHAPTER 3

BREAKING INTO THE BOYS' CLUB

You grin as you pilot the small airplane over the fields of eastern Washington. Ever since you were a little girl you've dreamed of flying. You overcame many obstacles to get your commercial pilot's license. Now, at age 24, you're trying to get your first job as a pilot.

A few moments later you touch down on an airstrip tucked among the fields. You glance at your passenger, who owns the plane and the airstrip. George hasn't seemed sure he wanted a female pilot working for him. You're taking him on a test drive to show him you're up to the job.

"You'll do," he says, and you let out a cheer.

Turn the page.

43

In the office, George nods in your direction and says to his wife, Ellie, "She can handle crop-dusting jobs or flying lessons."

Ellie smiles. "Good, because I just got a call from someone wanting lessons. I said he could start tomorrow."

You say, "He? Will a man mind taking lessons from a woman?"

"Couldn't say," Ellie replies. "I just told him to show up at 9:00 a.m."

As you leave, Ellie hands you something. It's today's paper: August 19, 1960. Ellie circled a headline that says, "Doctor Claims Women Would Make Good Astronauts."

"Wow! I'll read this as soon as I get home!" You head for your dad's pickup truck, thinking, *Women astronauts?*

You know that seven men, all military jet pilots, were picked last year by the National Aeronautics and Space Administration (NASA) to be America's first space travelers. Everyone wonders which astronaut will be first into space—and whether he'll get there before the Soviet Union does. The Soviets were the first to send satellites and animals into space. Now they're planning to send people, too.

The article is about Dr. W. Randolph Lovelace, an expert on the effects of flying. He tested pilots for NASA when the astronauts were chosen. Lovelace has also tested a female pilot named Geraldine "Jerrie" Cobb, who passed with high marks. He runs a program called Woman in Space at his clinic in Albuquerque, New Mexico. Lovelace said, "We are already in a position to say that certain qualities of the female space pilot are preferable to those of her male colleagues."

Turn the page.

You can hardly believe it! For the rest of the day, you think about bigger things than your first job as a pilot.

But when you try to tell your parents about the article, they don't share your excitement.

Jerrie Cobb trains with the Gimbal Rig to learn to control the spin of a tumbling spacecraft.

"Imagine seeing Earth from space!" you say.

"Absolutely not!" your dad says. You know he's worried, so you don't remind him that you're now a grown-up who makes her own decisions.

"What will Tom say?" your mom wails. Your high-school sweetheart has been waiting for you to "outgrow this flying nonsense" and marry him. You love Tom, but you're not ready to be a farmer's wife—or to give up flying.

You drop the subject. Still, your thoughts keep turning to that clinic in New Mexico. Should you apply? But what if your parents are right? Asking for more information would give you time to think it over.

47

To apply for astronaut testing, turn to page 48.
To write for information, turn to page 50.

You write to Dr. Lovelace, describing your flight training and experience. A few weeks later you are invited to New Mexico for the first set of tests.

Now you have to break the news. You start with George, your boss.

"I can't hold the pilot job for you forever," George says. "But good luck."

Your parents aren't happy. But once they see that you're determined to follow your dream of spaceflight, they accept it. Your father even lets you drive his truck to New Mexico.

Tom doesn't take your news well, either. You tell him, "I might not get in. Dozens of male pilots tried out for NASA's program, but only seven were picked."

"So you're giving up everything for a long shot," Tom says. He leaves without saying good-bye. You feel terrible, but you have a lot to do. You want to be on the road in the morning.

On the drive south you wonder if you're doing the right thing. Just outside Rock Springs, Wyoming, you hear news from the rocket base at Cape Canaveral, Florida. Earlier in the day NASA launched a rocket carrying a probe called Pioneer P-30. The probe was supposed to orbit the moon, but something went wrong. The spacecraft crashed in the Indian Ocean.

It could have been me in a spacecraft instead of that probe, you think. Suddenly you're not sure you want to take the risk. You could turn around right now and go back home.

To keep going to New Mexico, turn to page 52.
To turn the truck around, turn to page 63.

A few weeks later you receive a response letter from one of Dr. Lovelace's assistants. As you read, you realize the Woman in Space program is more complicated than you expected.

For one thing, NASA has decided not to test women for astronaut training. Dr. Lovelace hopes to change this, but for now the program is unofficial. A famous woman pilot, Jacqueline "Jackie" Cochran, is funding it.

You'll have to pay your own travel costs. And the tests won't be easy. You'll have cold water shot into your ears to test your balance. You'll be locked in a sealed tank of water in the dark, to see how you handle isolation. And then there's the spaceflight simulator. In this test, you'll be strapped into a capsule that whips from side to side, moves up and down, and rolls 30 times each minute. You must use a hand control to guide the capsule out of these movements.

The letter ends with an invitation to apply in person in New Mexico.

You look up from the letter. Outside, sunlight sparkles on the plane you use for flying lessons and crop-dusting jobs. It will be years before you can buy a plane of your own—even longer if you spend your savings trying to get into astronaut training. The dream of being the first woman in space is powerful, but is it worth it?

After learning to fly in 1932, Jackie Cochran set many speed, altitude, and distance aviation records.

To accept the Lovelace Clinic's invitation, turn to page 52.
To decline the invitation, turn to page 64.

You get a room at a motel across from the Lovelace Clinic. The following morning you meet Dr. Lovelace and the doctors who will do the tests. It will take a week to complete the more than 80 medical and physical tests in the first round.

"These are the same tests taken by men who want to be astronauts," one of the doctors says. "If you pass, you can move on to the next set."

You meet regularly with another woman pilot, Claire, to talk about the testing experiences.

"Have you had the clay yet?" Claire asks on the second day.

"What is *that?*"

Claire laughs. "Some kind of goop they put on your head for the electroencephalograph." In that test, doctors fasten sensors called electrodes to your scalp to study your brain waves.

"It can't be worse than the stress test," y

That afternoon you rode an exercise bicycle at high speed until you were ready to collapse. The doctors studied how your heart and lungs acted under the pressure. Now your legs feel like two limp rubber bands.

The next morning starts with the tilt-table test. Strapped to a table, you lie flat for 15 minutes. Then the table is suddenly tilted upright. This makes you so dizzy that you pass out. When you wake up, you insist on trying again. This time you don't faint, although your head spins. Afterward you hang upside down for half an hour, wired to a machine that tracks how well your blood circulates in that position.

Turn the page.

For the next test, the doctor shoots a jet of ice-cold water into your ear. Instantly you're too dizzy to focus your eyes or move. The room whirls around you. You lean over and vomit.

"Don't worry," a nurse tells you. "You'll be fine in a moment." The test is designed to see how well you handle vertigo, or an extreme loss of balance. You didn't handle it very well. And your ear still hurts minutes later.

The doctor says, "We can try again tomorrow. For now, get some rest."

As you walk back to the motel, you think, *do I have what it takes to pass these tests?*

But Claire's day was even worse. "Have you had the test where you blow through tubes while they listen to the blood flowing through your heart?" she asks. You nod.

"I failed," Claire says miserably. "They found a tiny flaw in my heart. Here on Earth it's nothing. But in space, if the capsule suddenly lost air pressure, that weak place in my heart could explode. I'm out of the program."

As Claire packs, a wave of homesickness washes over you. Should you leave, too?

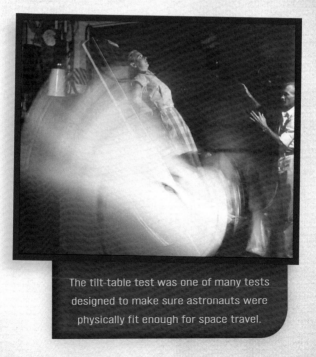

The tilt-table test was one of many tests designed to make sure astronauts were physically fit enough for space travel.

To take the ear test again tomorrow, turn to page 56.
To leave the program and go home, turn to page 65.

You try the ear test again. This time you don't vomit. After a few minutes the room stops spinning. You can follow commands such as, "Raise your right hand." Everyone gets dizzy, the doctor explains. The important thing is how long it takes you to recover.

At the end of the week you learn that you have passed the first round. The next round will take place at a military base with a spaceflight simulator. It will take months to arrange. For now, you can return to your job at the airstrip.

On April 12 the following spring, you are listening to the radio when you hear news that stuns you: "The Soviet Union has sent the first man into space. According to reports from Moscow, cosmonaut Yuri Gagarin, in the spacecraft *Vostok 1*, orbited Earth and returned safely."

Your telephone rings. It is Claire, calling from her home in Pennsylvania. "Did you hear?" she says. "The Soviets beat us again!"

"We'll show them," you tell her. "The first woman in space will be an American!"

On May 5, astronaut Alan Shepard becomes the first American in space. He doesn't orbit Earth, but he does fly his spacecraft. This is a first, because Gagarin's spacecraft flew mostly by remote control.

In July 1961 you receive a letter from Dr. Lovelace. Spaceflight simulator tests for the women pilots will take place in September at a U.S. Navy school in Pensacola, Florida. Once again you have to ask George for time away from your job. You also spend a chunk of your savings on a plane ticket. You're packing for the trip when a telegram arrives for you.

Turn the page.

It's news from Dr. Lovelace: "Regret to advise arrangements at Pensacola have been canceled."

Shocked, you sit down on your bed. You have no idea why the program stopped and when—or if—it will continue.

Later you learn that the other women who passed the first round of tests received identical telegrams. For some, the shock was even greater than it was for you. Several of them had quit their jobs because they couldn't get time off for the tests.

The program stopped because the Navy school won't use its equipment for an astronaut program that is not run by NASA. Dr. Lovelace is busy with other NASA projects and has given up on Woman in Space.

But pilot Jerrie Cobb hasn't given up. She talks to NASA officials and other members of the government about training women astronauts. In February 1962 she writes to you and the other women who had qualified for astronaut training, "I intend to keep hammering and trust that you are all still behind me."

Months later Cobb writes that she will speak before a Congressional committee on the question of women in space. The hearing will take place on July 17. It may be the last chance for the program you were so proud to join.

To go to Washington, D.C., for the hearing, turn to page 60.
To stay home, turn to page 66.

When you arrive in Washington, you meet Jerrie Cobb for the first time. The next day you take a seat in the audience for the "special hearing" on astronaut selection.

Cobb tells the nine men and two women on the committee that the women pilots who passed Dr. Lovelace's tests had results as good as those of the male astronauts. She says, "We [women] seek, only, a place in our nation's space future without discrimination . . . There were women on the Mayflower and on the first wagon trains west, working alongside the men to forge new trails to new vistas. We ask that opportunity in the pioneering of space." She also calls NASA's focus on military test pilots unfair to women because the armed services don't let women fly jet planes.

Astronaut John Glenn, who last February became the first American to orbit Earth, also speaks. He says that test-pilot experience is vital to astronauts. Women will have a place in space exploration, he says—just not now.

The committee chairman says, "I think the loss of prestige in losing a woman in space would certainly be something that we would hear about." *In other words,* you think angrily, *women need to be "protected." Just another way of saying "kept out of the boys' club."*

John Glenn orbited Earth three times in his historic flight. It lasted 4 hours and 56 minutes.

Turn the page.

At the end of the day, the committee decides against training women astronauts. More than a year earlier, on May 25, 1961, President John F. Kennedy had told Congress, "I believe that this nation should commit itself to achieving the goal, before this decade is out, of landing a man on the moon and returning him safely to the Earth." The committee wants NASA to spend its time and money on the moon goal.

You are crushed, but as you leave the room, you overhear NASA employees talking about jobs in the agency's national headquarters. Working for NASA, you'd still be part of the space program in a small way.

To return to your piloting job, turn to page 66.
To work for NASA, turn to page 67.

It's hard to admit that you changed your mind, but your parents are thrilled to see you. George welcomes you back to the airstrip. Even Tom comes around after you have been home for a few days.

Two years later you and Tom have been married for almost a year. You're no longer flying, but you keep busy with a house of your own and a baby on the way.

Over the years you watch rocket launches and spaceflights on TV with your children. When they talk about astronauts, you tell them to follow their dreams.

THE END

To follow another path, turn to page 11.
To read the conclusion, turn to page 101.

You write back to Dr. Lovelace's clinic to say that you've decided not to apply. For just a moment, you wonder if you've missed the chance to do something heroic. All you know for sure, though, is that you won't risk your flying career.

Four years later you get a job as a pilot for a charity that sends food and medicine to people suffering from disasters such as famines and floods. Over the years you make hundreds of life-saving flights in countries around the world.

You rejoice in 1978 when NASA accepts the first women into astronaut training. Even though you are now too old to apply, you feel proud knowing that American women will finally make the leap into space.

THE END

To follow another path, turn to page 11.
To read the conclusion, turn to page 101.

You decide that you can't put your life on hold for a dream that might not come true. So you thank Dr. Lovelace and his staff and say good-bye.

"Women will go to space someday," one of the doctors says. "You and everyone else who took part in this program will have helped."

You carry that thought with you as you make the long drive home. You hope that it's not too late to return to your job at the airstrip. At least you will always have flying.

THE END

To follow another path, turn to page 11.
To read the conclusion, turn to page 101.

A year after you return to work at the airstrip, George turns the business over to his son, Jeff. Although Jeff isn't a pilot, he has friends who learned to fly in the Air Force. He hires them for giving lessons and spraying crops. You find yourself out of a job.

You move from your small town to a larger city, Seattle, hoping that it will offer a piloting opportunity. To pay your bills, you take a job in a real-estate office. Soon you marry and start a family. When your children are teenagers, you update your pilot's license and buy a small plane. Now you operate your own business, carrying people and mail to remote islands off the Pacific coast.

THE END

To follow another path, turn to page 11.
To read the conclusion, turn to page 101.

Working as a file clerk for NASA is a lot less exciting than flying. At first you wonder if you made a mistake. But as you explore Washington D.C.'s museums and monuments, you find that you enjoy big-city life.

Soon after you start, new machines called computers are brought to your office. Some of the older employees want nothing to do with them, but you volunteer to learn how to use them. Within months you're training other employees in computer skills.

Turn the page.

By early 1963 you have already been promoted to a higher-level job, overseeing how records are stored. In June, when a former Soviet factory worker named Valentina Tereshkova becomes the first woman in space, a coworker says to you, "Say, weren't you part of that program to train women astronauts?"

Sally Ride worked the space shuttle's robotic arm on her first space mission.

Everyone wants to hear the details.

"What a shame the politicians killed that program!" someone exclaims. "Now the Soviets have scored another win."

"We'll send a woman to space someday," you reply.

Twenty years later, you're the manager of the NASA office when the space shuttle *Challenger* is launched. You watch as the rocket carrying the shuttle and its five crew members lifts off on June 18, 1983.

This launch holds special meaning to you. One crew member is Sally Ride, the first American woman in space.

THE END

To follow another path, turn to page 11.
To read the conclusion, turn to page 101.

Cosmonaut Valentina Tereshkova became the first woman in space on June 16, 1963.

CHAPTER 4

SOVIETS IN SPACE

You gaze out the train window. The landscape is covered with snow in March 1964, but your military service is ending and your spirits are high. Soon you will see your wife, Anya, and 5-year-old daughter, Sasha.

Sitting with Anya in the family's small Moscow apartment, you explain that you've been offered two jobs. "Both involving space exploration!" you say.

You are proud of the many Soviet triumphs in space, such as the first satellite and the first man in space. Last year the Soviet Union set two new records: first woman in space and longest time spent in space—three days.

Turn the page.

"What are these jobs?" Anya asks.

One job is with a government-run rocketry design project in Moscow. It would be a low-level job at first. Your engineering education is basic. But you can learn quickly, and you have experience as a jet pilot from your military service. This earns you a place on a design team.

"And the other job—?" your wife asks.

You answer with a single word: "Cosmonaut."

She throws her arms around you. "I'm proud of you! But it's so dangerous!"

You have been bursting with excitement at the thought of becoming a cosmonaut, one of the few who can travel into space. Cosmonauts are heroes, admired by all. At the same time, you understand your wife's fears. Riding into airless, cold space atop a blazing rocket is risky.

In an engineering job, you'll help build the rockets that carry cosmonauts and satellites to space. Your family will stay in Moscow. In a year or two you'll be able to afford your own apartment—although the waiting list for apartments is long.

If you become a cosmonaut, you and your family will move to Star City, the new cosmonaut training center outside Moscow. The best part of this job is the chance to go into space, but you know that many cosmonauts are never chosen for space missions. If you are chosen for a space mission, you'll deal with dangers that no engineer would face.

To become a cosmonaut, turn to page 74.
To become a rocket engineer, turn to page 80.

Your family settles into a small apartment in Star City, northeast of Moscow. Anya goes to work as a teacher's helper, and Sasha starts school.

You are assigned to a group of cosmonauts training for the new *Voskhod* spacecraft. It's a version of the *Vostok* craft that carried Yuri Gagarin and Valentina Tereshkova into space. *Vostok* has been retired. Everyone believes that the next cosmonauts sent into space will be aboard a *Voskhod* craft.

Your training includes three stages. One is exercise and medical testing. Another is flight practice, to sharpen your piloting skills. The third is studying the spacecraft and how it works. Your engineering studies help here. You soon understand *Voskhod*'s mechanical and electrical systems.

Voskhod has two sections: a ball-shaped capsule 7.9 feet (2.4 m) across, and an engine attached to the capsule. A large rocket will boost the *Voskhod* into space. The engine on the capsule will brake the capsule when it returns to Earth.

The capsule is similar to the *Vostok*, except for the ejection seat. As *Vostok* returned to Earth, the cosmonaut ejected out of the capsule on a seat, then floated to the ground with a parachute. In *Voskhod*, the seat is replaced by three couches. The goal is to be the first to send more than one traveler to space in a single capsule. The capsule is so crowded that its crew can't wear space suits. The crew will return to Earth inside *Voskhod*, hoping that its braking engine and parachutes work. If the capsule loses air pressure, the lack of space suits will kill the cosmonauts.

Turn the page.

You are secretly relieved not to be chosen for the first Voskhod mission, in October 1964. To everyone's surprise, the three-man crew is changed just three days before the mission. You hear that the change was political. Two of the replacements are not pilots, but they have supporters in the government. At least the cosmonaut in command, Vladimir Komarov, is a trained pilot. Another rumor says that the capsule is so cramped that the crew had to go on crash diets to fit inside.

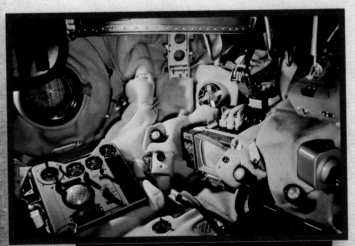

The cabin of *Voskhod 1* was so small that the cosmonauts could not wear space suits.

Voskhod 1 is launched from the Baikonur Cosmodrome, a rocket base in central Asia. Along with the other cosmonauts and their families, you wait for more than a day as the spacecraft orbits Earth. When it returns safely with the cosmonauts alive, the Soviet government announces its latest space triumph to the world.

Now the pressure is on for *Voskhod 2*. This capsule will have an air lock so that a cosmonaut can leave the craft for a short space walk. Because the space walker must put on a space suit, the capsule will have a two-person crew.

Once again, you aren't chosen. Instead you help the cosmonauts practice with the air lock and space suits. The launch on March 18, 1965, is a success. Cosmonaut Alexey Leonov makes the first space walk, spending 10 minutes outside the spacecraft. That's when the trouble starts.

Turn the page.

In the airlessness of space, Leonov's space suit unexpectedly puffs up. It becomes so stiff that he can't bend his arms and legs to get back into the air lock. He must let oxygen out of his suit—a dangerous thing to do, because losing too much oxygen could be deadly. Leonov makes it back inside, but the cosmonauts have trouble sealing the door to the air lock. The spacecraft begins its return to Earth. But it's so crowded that the cosmonauts take 46 seconds longer than planned to get into their couches. This delay, and a problem with the spacecraft's guidance system, forces the crew to change course.

Voskhod 2 misses its landing zone. Mission controllers don't know where the capsule landed, or whether the cosmonauts survived. The call goes out for volunteers to go out in search planes. You want to help, but you worry because you did some of the space-suit training. If Leonov is alive, maybe he'll blame you. That could destroy your future in the highly political cosmonaut program.

The first space walk was another victory for the Soviets in the space race.

To join the search party, turn to page 82.
To stay home and hope no one connects you with the disaster, turn to page 92.

You discover that the Soviet space program isn't easy to understand. There are four different design groups. Each has a chief designer and its own plans for spacecraft and missions. These groups compete fiercely for government money and attention.

The two most important chief designers are Sergei Korolev and Vladimir Chelomei. You can become a junior engineer for either of them.

Korolev has had a remarkable career. Trained as a pilot and an engineer, he launched the Soviet Union's first liquid-fueled rocket in 1933. Later he led the design office responsible for the first satellite, Sputnik, and the first space traveler, Yuri Gagarin. Korolev wants to send cosmonauts to the moon. Instead, he has been ordered to focus on missions closer to Earth, using his *Voskhod* spacecraft.

Chelomei is a good scientist and a friend of Nikita Khrushchev , one of the top two political leaders of the Soviet Union. Chelomei has less experience than Korolev in designing spacecraft and managing large projects, but he's just been put in charge of the moon-landing program.

Sergei Korolev is credited with much of the Soviet Union's success in space exploration.

To work under Korolev, turn to page 86.
To join Chelomei's office, turn to page 94.

You fly one of several planes that soon locate the lost *Voskhod 2* in a forested, snow-covered area 240 miles (386 km) from the landing zone. Trees and rocky ground prevent you from landing. Mission controllers decide to land helicopters as close as possible. From there, rescuers will ski to the capsule.

You join the ski group. The next day, you and half a dozen other rescuers reach the capsule. The cosmonauts are alive, but they spent a miserable night. The capsule's heater is broken and its door blown open. The howls of wolves drifted in the freezing air. But Leonov greets you with a clap on the shoulder and friendly words: "Things don't always go as planned, right, comrade?"

Night is coming, so you help build a shelter and a big fire. In the morning, rescuers and cosmonauts ski out to the waiting helicopter.

Afterward, your place in the cosmonaut program seems safe. You wonder if Leonov put in a good word for you. *Voskhod*, however, is retired. The next cosmonauts will ride a different spacecraft, the brand-new *Soyuz*. You are thrilled by this news, because the goal of the Soyuz program is to land a cosmonaut on the moon!

A moon landing will be a huge win in the space race. The Americans have a goal to do it by the end of the 1960s. You dream of beating them there.

In February 1966, the unmanned Soviet spacecraft Luna 9 makes the first soft landing on the moon. The successful mission helps show that a spacecraft can land on the moon without killing its passengers.

Turn the page.

In January 1967, you learn of a tragedy in the American space program. Three astronauts die in a fire while their spacecraft is being tested on the ground. You're no fan of the U.S. program, but you and the other cosmonauts are sad about the deaths. At the same time, you're shocked that the United States is so open with the news. Russia keeps quiet about its space failures. Missions are revealed to the world only after they succeed.

The *Soyuz* spacecraft is tested with several unmanned flights before the first cosmonaut mission, *Soyuz 1*, is scheduled for April. The capsule will carry Vladimir Komarov, who had been aboard *Voskhod 1*. Yuri Gagarin, the first person in space, is Komarov's backup. You're proud and nervous when you're named as the second backup. If neither Komarov nor Gagarin can fly, you'll go into space.

Soyuz 1 takes off as planned, with Komarov aboard. It's supposed to dock with a second spacecraft—something never done before. Bad weather prevents the second craft from launching, and Komarov has trouble with the electrical system on Soyuz 1. Mission control decides to bring him down early. After 18 orbits in little more than a day, Soyuz 1 starts to descend, but its four parachutes fail to work. Instead of a soft landing, Soyuz 1 crashes to Earth and bursts into flames, killing Komarov. He is the first person to die in spaceflight.

You are deeply shaken. *What if it had been me?* you think. You must make a decision.

To remain in the cosmonaut program, turn to page 88.
To leave the program, turn to page 93.

Korolev juggles many projects. In 1964 he's under pressure to give the Soviet Union more space firsts. His answer is the *Voskhod*, a spacecraft that can carry more than one cosmonaut. A cosmonaut in his *Voskhod 2* makes the first space walk in 1965—although the mission nearly ends in disaster when the capsule lands off course. Meanwhile, you've been assigned to a group planning the next Soviet spacecraft, *Soyuz*. Korolev hopes that the *Soyuz* spacecraft and his large N1 rocket will take cosmonauts to the moon.

When Korolev dies suddenly in 1966, you worry about your future in the space program. Fortunately, Vasili Mishin, who takes Korolev's place, has faith in *Soyuz* and the N1. Your project remains important, and you feel the pressure from above for a successful mission.

In early 1967 you learn that a cosmonaut will go into space in *Soyuz 1* in April. You think it's too soon. There were problems with the unmanned test flights of *Soyuz*. Because it isn't wise to criticize high-level decisions, you talk this over with Dmitri, your most trusted colleague.

"You're right, we haven't had time to check it thoroughly," Dmitri agrees. Yet when you say that the engineers should speak up, he refuses. "I can't call that kind of attention to myself," he says.

To tell your superiors that the launch should be postponed, turn to page 97.

To say nothing but keep working on the spacecraft, turn to page 98.

You say nothing about your fear of being sent to space. But you wonder if your superiors know about it. The years go by and you're never chosen for a spaceflight.

Often you're sent to schools and factories to make public appearances or speeches about the space program, giving the Soviet people a chance to see a cosmonaut. You also help train new cosmonauts in piloting skills and the use of space suits.

Soviet cosmonauts performed weightlessness training in airplanes.

In January 1969, you watch nervously as three men you trained ride into space aboard the *Soyuz 5* spacecraft. It docks in space with *Soyuz 4*, the first time such a thing has been done. Wearing space suits, two cosmonauts leave the *Soyuz 5* capsule and return to Earth in *Soyuz 4*. You're proud of your part in this successful mission.

But just six months later, the Soviet space program suffers a crushing defeat. The American spacecraft *Apollo 11* lands on the moon on July 20, 1969. Astronaut Neil Armstrong becomes the first person to set foot on the moon. In spite of the many Soviet firsts in space, people around the world see the moon landing as the biggest victory of the space race.

Turn the page.

As a cosmonaut, you know something that most of the world doesn't know. Earlier that year, two N1 rockets, built to carry cosmonauts to the moon, exploded during test launches. The Soviet moon program is going nowhere. The space program has a new goal: a space station in orbit around Earth. It achieves that goal in 1971 with the first manned station, Salyut 1.

By the next year, the tensions of the Cold War are beginning to ease. U.S. president Richard Nixon and Soviet premier Leonid Brezhnev agree to plan a shared space mission. An American *Apollo* spacecraft and a Soviet *Soyuz* craft will dock in space. Astronauts and cosmonauts will exchange visits.

The shared mission is scheduled in 1975. By that time, you've been a cosmonaut for more than 10 years. Your daughter, Sasha, has spent two-thirds of her life in Star City. Your life is a comfortable routine—until you are named as a backup for one of the cosmonauts on the shared mission.

"Do you think you'll have to go?" Anya asks.

"I don't know. But this time, I'm ready."

But you're not called on to make the spaceflight. The Apollo-Soyuz shared mission is a success. It also marks an end to the space race.

Although you never go to space, you spend the rest of your career in the cosmonaut program. You remain proud of your country's triumphs in space.

THE END

To follow another path, turn to page 11.
To read the conclusion, turn to page 101.

You feel guilty for not helping to look for the missing cosmonauts. But you remind yourself that your wife and Sasha depend on you. You can't risk losing your place in the program.

The *Voskhod 2* is located, and the cosmonauts are rescued. You're happy at the news, but just three days later you receive a notice that you're being released from the cosmonaut program. Arrangements are being made to send you and your family back to Moscow.

Stunned, you try to find out why. Were you unfairly linked to the space-suit problem, as you feared? Or was it because you didn't volunteer for the search-and-rescue mission? No one will tell you. You, Anya, and Sasha pack for the journey back to your parents' apartment, wondering what you'll do next.

THE END

To follow another path, turn to page 11.
To read the conclusion, turn to page 101.

You tell your superiors that you don't want to go into space. They remind you that going to space would be a service to your country. You explain that your concern for your family might keep you from doing the best possible job. You ask to work as an engineer or to train other cosmonauts. Instead, your supervisors tell you that you'll take a job teaching basic engineering— at a small school in eastern Russia. You know you're being sent far away so that your story can never leak out to American newspapers.

As your family begins the long train ride to your new home, you ask Anya, "Do you think I'm a coward for quitting?"

She takes your hand and says, "I think it is the bravest thing you have ever done."

THE END

To follow another path, turn to page 11.
To read the conclusion, turn to page 101.

In March 1964 you join Chelomei's design office. You're put on a team that is planning a lunar base. Your job is to design the systems that will give future cosmonauts air, water, light, and heat. It's a fascinating project, but you wonder if it's useful. The lunar program is making slow progress. It will be years before Chelomei can send a cosmonaut to the moon.

Chelomei doesn't have years. You've heard rumors that Leonid Brezhnev, chairman of the Soviet government, is plotting against Khrushchev, his rival. Six months after you go to work for Chelomei, Brezhnev calls Khrushchev back from vacation for an urgent government session. Brezhnev's backers tell Khrushchev he should resign. Khrushchev quits, and Chelomei has lost his top supporter.

The lunar program is given to Korolev's design office. But Korolev isn't interested in your group's long-range plan for a moon base. Yet Chelomei is not out of a job, and neither are you. The Soviet military has always been a driving force behind your country's space programs. Now the military wants Chelomei to continue working on a large rocket he is designing, the Proton. Chelomei picks you as part of the team developing the Proton's engines.

Before long Proton rockets are used to launch both military and scientific Soviet satellites. Chelomei regains some power in 1970, when he is given the space-station program. The following year a Proton rocket launches the first space station with a crew, Salyut 1.

Turn the page.

From Baikonur, the Soviet rocket base in central Asia, you watch the launch. Then you go back to Moscow to work on the next set of Salyut space stations. You're relieved to still have a job in your country's space program.

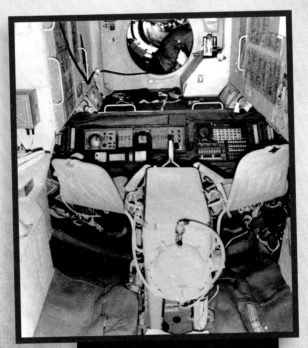

Inside the Salyut 1 space station.

THE END

To follow another path, turn to page 11.
To read the conclusion, turn to page 101.

You approach your senior engineer with your worries. You are not alone, it seems. Several top engineers warn Mishin and the government that *Soyuz* isn't ready for a manned flight. They are overruled. The launch takes place as planned. As the capsule is returning to Earth, its parachutes fail to work. *Soyuz 1* crashes in a fireball, killing cosmonaut Vladimir Komarov.

The disaster shakes up Mishin and his entire staff. Your senior engineer is invited to transfer to a position building and testing military rockets. You decide to go with him. You may not send a Soviet cosmonaut to the moon, but at least you will be able to take pride in your job.

THE END

To follow another path, turn to page 11.
To read the conclusion, turn to page 101.

Like Dmitri, you say nothing about your fear that the *Soyuz* might not be ready for a manned flight. After cosmonaut Vladimir Komarov dies in the crash of *Soyuz 1*, you are eaten up by guilt. "I should have done something!" you tell Anya.

Vladimir Komarov

"Others tried," she says. "They failed. You would have failed, too."

"What should I do now?"

She says, "Be a good engineer. Make *Soyuz* as good as it can be, so that no one else dies."

You spend the rest of your career working on the Soyuz series of spacecraft. *Soyuz* becomes the world's most reliable spacecraft design. It carries cosmonauts to the Salyut and Mir space stations. Even after the Soviet Union breaks up into separate countries in 1991, the *Soyuz* keeps working, carrying space travelers from many nations to the International Space Station.

THE END

To follow another path, turn to page 11.
To read the conclusion, turn to page 101.

100

Astronauts Edwin "Buzz" Aldrin (pictured) and
Neil Armstrong were the first humans to walk on the moon.

CHAPTER 5

THE END OF THE RACE

Both the Soviet Union and the United States had wins and losses in the space race. The Soviet Union had a big win when it sent the first satellite, Sputnik, into orbit in 1957. Two years later the Soviets launched the first spacecraft to reach the moon. Two years after that they sent the first human, cosmonaut Yuri Gagarin, into space.

Alarmed by the Soviet successes, the United States stepped up its own space program. Throughout the 1960s the Americans worked toward the goal of landing astronauts on the moon. The moon landing in 1969 was the biggest U.S. win of the space race.

The Soviet Union tried several times to send cosmonauts to the moon, but failed. Instead the Soviet program turned its attention to space stations. It launched the first human-staffed space station in 1971.

A new era in space began a year later. U.S. president Richard Nixon and Soviet premier Leonid Brezhnev agreed to cooperate on a shared space mission. In 1975 an American *Apollo* spacecraft docked with a Soviet *Soyuz* spacecraft. The crews visited each other's ships and did science experiments together. The space race was over. But Cold War tensions lingered until 1991, when the Soviet Union broke into 15 independent countries.

The space race did more than send satellites into space and land astronauts on the moon. It led to breakthroughs in science and technology that have shaped people's everyday lives. Products that were invented or improved for use in space include satellite TV, video game joysticks, portable computers, ear thermometers, lightweight building materials, solar panels, water filters, and the Global Positioning System (GPS) software found in phones and cars.

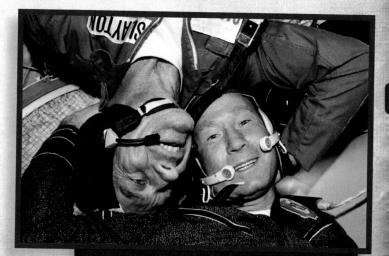

Astronaut Donald Slayton (left) and cosmonaut Aleksey Leonov (right) embraced when their crews met in orbit on July 17, 1975.

The space race also gripped the public imagination. It started just as TVs came into wide use. Millions of people watched rocket launches and broadcasts from space on TV. The early astronauts and cosmonauts were public heroes.

For a long time, the United States and the Soviet Union were the only nations with space programs. Today people from many countries travel to the International Space Station, carried into space on Russian rockets. The United States, Russia, China, India, Japan, and the European Space Agency (ESA) all have active space programs. The space race may be over, but space exploration is just beginning.

On April 12, 2016, ESA astronaut Tim Peake
tweeted a picture of himself aboard the
International Space Station (ISS) reading
Yuri Gagarin's autobiography.

TIMELINE

1945 World War II ends. The United States and the Soviet Union acquire V-2 missiles and scientists from defeated Germany.

1955 The United States and the Soviet Union each announce plans to launch a satellite to orbit Earth.

1957 On October 4, the Soviet Union launches the first artificial satellite, Sputnik 1. On November 3, the Soviet Union sends a dog into space in Sputnik 2. On December 6, the first U.S. attempt to launch a satellite, using a Vanguard rocket, fails.

1958 On January 31, the first U.S. satellite, Explorer 1, is successfully launched. On July 29, President Dwight D. Eisenhower creates the National Aeronautics and Space Administration (NASA).

1959 The unmanned Soviet spacecraft Luna 2 is first to reach the moon. Luna 3 takes the first pictures of the far side of the moon. NASA chooses the first seven U.S. astronauts.

1960 The first Mercury-Redstone launch fails due to a faulty electrical plug. The Woman in Space program begins, not sponsored by NASA.

1961 On April 12, Soviet cosmonaut Yuri Gagarin is the first person in space. On May 5, astronaut Alan Shepard is the first American in space and first to fully control a spacecraft, the *Freedom 7*. President John F. Kennedy says that the U.S. should send an astronaut to the moon by the end of the 1960s.

1963 Soviet cosmonaut Valentina Tereshkova becomes the first woman in space.

1964 Three Soviet cosmonauts on *Voskhod 1* are the first multiperson crew in space.

1965 A Soviet cosmonaut on *Voskhod 2* makes the first space walk.

1966 Soviet spacecraft Luna 9 makes the first soft landing on the moon.

1967 The American and Soviet space programs experience disasters that kill three astronauts and a cosmonaut.

1969 U.S. spacecraft *Apollo 11* carries the first people to land on the moon and returns them to Earth.

1971 Soviet Salyut 1 is the first space station with a crew.

1972 The Soviet Union and the United States agree to plan a shared space mission.

1975 The United States and the Soviet Union carry out the Apollo-Soyuz mission, bringing together Soviet cosmonauts and American astronauts. The space race ends.

OTHER PATHS TO EXPLORE

In this book, you've seen how events from the past look different from three points of view. Perspectives on history are as varied as the people who lived it. Seeing history from many points of view is an important part of understanding it. Here are ideas for other space race points of view to explore.

- Putting satellites and people into space cost the United States billions of dollars. Some Americans did not believe that this was the best way for the country to spend its money. Were the benefits of the space race worth the cost? Explain why or why not.
  (Integration of Knowledge and Ideas)

- The space race was a scientific and technical competition between the world's two superpowers, the United States and the Soviet Union, but it was also a political competition. How did other nations regard this activity? What did leaders and people in countries such as China, France, Great Britain, or Egypt think about the space race? Did they care who won? If so, why? Refer to outside sources for your answer.
  (Integration of Knowledge and Ideas)

READ MORE

Hubbard, Ben. *Yuri Gagarin and the Race to Space.* Chicago: Heinemann-Raintree, 2016.

Lassieur, Allison. *The Race to the Moon: An Interactive History Adventure.* North Mankato, Minn.: Capstone Press, 2014.

Parker, Steve. *Race to the Moon.* Mankato, Minn.: A+, Smart Apple Media, 2016.

Wilkinson, Philip. *Spacebusters: The Race to the Moon.* New York: DK Pub., 2012.

INTERNET SITES

FactHound offers a safe, fun way to find Internet sites related to this book. All of the sites on FactHound have been researched by our staff.

Here's all you do:

Visit *www.facthound.com*

Type in this code: 9781491481011

GLOSSARY

air lock (AYR-LOK)—enclosure between two airtight doors to permit passage from one space to the other.

astronaut (AS-truh-nawt)—a person who is trained to live and work in space

atmosphere (AT-muhss-fihr)—the mixture of gases that surrounds the Earth

atomic bomb (uh-TOM-ik BOM)—weapon that uses nuclear power to create massive destruction

ballistic missile (buh-LISS-tik MISS-uhl)—a missile that is powered as it climbs, but falls freely

civilian (si-VIL-yuhn)—a person who is not in the military

communism (KAHM-yuh-ni-zuhm)—a way of organizing a country so that all the land, houses, and factories belong to the government, and the profits are shared by all

cosmonaut (KAHZ-moh-nawt)—a Soviet astronaut

drag (DRAG)—the force that resists the motion of an object moving through the air

electroencephalograph (i-lek-troh-en-SEF-uh-loh-graf)—device for detecting and recording brain waves

engineer (en-juh-NEER)—a person who uses science and math to plan, design, or build

lunar (LOO-nur)—having to do with a moon

satellite (SAT-uh-lite)—an object that moves around a planet or other cosmic body

BIBLIOGRAPHY

Biddle, Wayne. *Dark Side of the Moon: Wernher von Braun, the Third Reich, and the Space Race*. New York: W. W. Norton, 2009.

Bille, Matthew, and Erika Lishock. *The First Space Race: Launching the World's First Satellites*. College Station, Tex.: Texas A&M University Press, 2004.

Brzezinski, Matthew. *Red Moon Rising: Sputnik and the Hidden Rivalries that Ignited the Space Age*. New York: Times Books, 2007.

Cadbury, Deborah. *Space Race: The Epic Battle between America and the Soviet Union for Dominion of Space*. New York: HarperCollins, 2006.

D'Antonio, Michael. *A Ball, a Dog, and a Monkey: 1957—The Space Race Begins*. New York: Simon & Schuster, 2007.

Gerovitch, Slava. *Voices of the Soviet Space Program: Cosmonauts, Soldiers, and Engineers Who Took the USSR into Space*. New York: Palgrave Macmillan, 2014.

Harford, James. *Korolev: How One Man Masterminded the Soviet Drive to Beat America to the Moon*. New York: Wiley, 1997.

Nolen, Stephanie. *Promised the Moon: The Untold Story of the First Women in the Space Race*. New York: Four Walls Eight Windows, 2003.

Weitekamp, Margaret A. *Right Stuff, Wrong Sex: America's First Women in Space Program*. Baltimore: Johns Hopkins University Press, 2004.

INDEX